The Power of God

Dreams, Visions, Miracles, Testimonies, and Signs and Wonders

by

Annie M. Burton

Copyright © 2022 Annie M. Burton

All rights reserved. No part of this publication may be reproduced, distributed, or transmitted in any form or by any means, including photocopying, recording, or other electronic or mechanical methods, without the prior written permission of the publisher, except in the case of brief quotations embodied in critical reviews and certain other noncommercial uses permitted by copyright law.

ISBN-31. 978-1-951300-39-5

Liberation's Publishing LLC
West Point - Mississippi

The Power of God

Dreams, Visions, Miracles, Testimonies, and Signs and Wonders

Contents

Preface 1
Part One 3
   The Power of The Person of God 5
   The Power of God 7
   My First Miracle: Healed of a Brain Tumor 9
   Street Meetings: The Making of a Church 12
The Ones Who Made a Difference 14
   Sister Georgia Ryan 14
   Mother Ruby Paden 16
   Missionary Cherry Scott 18
   Holiness Is Right: My Next Miracle 20
   Filled with The Holy Ghost: My Third Miracle 22
   Mother Artelia Shannon Kelly 25
   Brother Will Womack 27
   Mother Lula Meeks 29
   Mother Nellie Chambers 30
   Mother Pearl Allen 31
   Sunday School 33
   Mrs. Pollye Walker 34
   Mrs. Larrenia Moore 35
   Mrs. Everlena Christian 37
Part Two Dreams and Visions 39
   Dreams and Visions 41
   My First Vision 42
   My Next Vision 43
   Signs and Wonders 44
   Angels in The House 45
   Beheading Demons 46
   Home Coming 47
   My First Vision of an Infant 49
   A Vision of Water Underground 50

Fire Burning Underneath My Feet	51
The Voice of The Lord	52
The Spirit of God Flowing Like a River	53
Miracles of The Century	54
A Double Family Miracle	55
A Miracle in Alligator Mississippi	57
A Miracle Baby	58
The Explosion of the Red Panther in Clarksdale	59
The Unexpected	60
Part Three	62
Honoring Bishop Timothy Titus Scott	64
Bishop Dr. T. D. Lockett	69
Bishop T D Lockett Ministering Under the Anointing	71
About the Author	73

Dedication

I dedicate this book to the memory of my parents, Warren Sr, and Larrenia Gholston Moore and to my grandparents, Anthony and Roxie Parker Gholston and Will and Anna Harden Moore. Gone but not forgotten. To God be the glory for the things He has done!

Preface

The Lord inspired me to write this book to remind some and inform others to remember where we came from, and how we arrived to where we are today. It's the power of God. He's our only source. All blessings come from him. I feel the need to encourage more people to believe in God like never before.

The things I've seen and experienced in the spiritual realm I'm expressing in this book will make a believer of many. I've seen the spirit of God on other people as they ministered to the people of God and experienced the Holy Spirit within me. Some things that I can't tell. I thank God for revealing himself to me in visions, signs, and wonders and revelation knowledge in my walk with him.

"The LORD answered me, and said, Write the vision, and make it plain upon tables, that he may run that readeth it. For the vision is yet for an appointed time, but at the end it shall speak, and not lie: though it tarry, wait for it; because it will surely come, it will not tarry." Habakkuk 2:2-3

Part One

The Power of The Person of God

Habakkuk 3:3-4 God came from Teman, and the Holy One from mount Paran. Selah. His glory covered the heavens, and the earth was full of his praise. 4-And his brightness was as the light: he has horns coming out of his hands and there was the hiding of his power. KJV

God is sovereign. We can't understand his work by natural thinking alone. Faith must rest in God's love and our knowledge of him. Sovereignty means that God is all powerful. He knows all. He is everywhere present, and his decision is final. God is the author of all the Praise and Power of the Universe.

Reference Scriptures

Jeremiah 10:10 But the Lord is the true God, he is the living God, and an everlasting King: at his wrath, the earth shall tremble, and the nations shall not be able to abide his indignation. KJV

Daniel 4:17 This matter is by the decree of the watchers, and the demand by the word of the holy ones to intent that the living may know that the most High ruleth in the Kingdom of men and giveth it to whomsoever he will and setteth up over it the basest of men. KJV

1 Samuel 2:8 He raiseth up the poor out of the dust and lifted up the beggar from the dunghill to set them among princes and to make them inherit the throne of glory: for the pillars of the earth are the Lord's and he hath set the world upon them. KJV

The Power of God

I thank God for his grace and mercy I thank him for forgiving me of my sins. He is almighty. I am saved by grace through faith. It is the gift of God. He sent his son; His name is Jesus He came to seek and save that which was lost.

God is awesome in all of his ways. He is our source. It is in him that we live and move and have our being. God is truly amazing. Jesus gave his life on the cross of calvary. He shed his blood and made the atonement, without the shedding of blood there is no remission of sin. The best miracle you can have is the gift of salvation, being saved from sin. God has the power to forgive sin.

When you are outside, just look up at the vastness of the Sky, his handywork. The creator of the Universe. His wisdom and knowledge are above our comprehension the works of his hands are there for all to see. Look up and know that there is a God in heaven. He is the governor of all nations. Get to know him in the power of his resurrection and in the fellowship of his love. Desire the gifts of the spirit and produce fruit.

My First Miracle: Healed of a Brain Tumor

In nineteen sixty-nine, I registered to enter the Practical Nurse program in my hometown and was accepted. I began attending classes in nineteen seventy. After my friend Freddie registered and told me about a program where you could get scholarship funds to buy books etc. I sought it out but was unable to get some of the assistance she talked about. But was determined to go on and get the training anyway. I was turned down by that Program director.

There were six of us, Five in Clarksdale and one in Charleston. I had transportation, but no income. So, they asked to ride with me. I said yes. My friend from Charleston would ride with someone and spend the night at my house and we would study together. They would buy gas, lunch, and pay for riding I had purchased a nineteen fifty-four Plymouth. The person was selling the car for one hundred fifty dollars. I only could come up with one hundred thirty-nine. They accepted the money and sold me the car. I used it when I was writing Insurance.

Things were going well at school. Then suddenly I became so ill I had to be admitted to the hospital. Then I was sent to Jackson to the University Hospital. They did a lot of testing and said I had a brain tumor the size of a golf ball and they wanted to operate. My head would hurt so bad I would get so sick to my stomach. I would take Tylenol. I remained there for one week. They wanted me to sign a form to consent for surgery. I said, "no." I refused to sign. They did not give me anything for pain. I took my own Tylenol. At that time, they used a saw to cut your skull. Laser surgery was unknown. I told the doctor that God was going to heal me. I was not going to have that surgery-so they let me go home. I caught the greyhound bus and came home, someone told me about a tent revival was going on and I said I was going that night.

So, I went to the tent meeting. The people were rejoicing, singing, dancing, and clapping their hands praising the Lord. I found a seat as close to the front as I could. After the preacher brought the message, people went up to the altar for different reasons. I came up to be healed. It was a white preacher that preached. He asked me what I wanted from the Lord. I told him the doctor told me I had a brain tumor the size of a golf ball and I wanted the Lord to heal me. He laid his hands on my head and began to pray for my healing. After a minute I began to rejoice. I started shouting and dancing and running. I almost ran out from under the tent into the street. They had to catch me. I was healed that night. My head did not hurt any more. I was not sick anymore. I went back to nursing school and finished and graduated on time. This was my first miracle. At that time, I didn't know that God was a healer. I wasn't saved, but God healed me anyway. I told the doctor that God was going to heal me, and he did just that. I never had to have any surgery. I thanked God for my miracle. God is a miracle working God.

Isaiah 53:4-5. Surely, he hath born our griefs and carried our sorrows: yet we did esteem him stricken, smitten of God and afflicted. But he was wounded for our transgressions he was bruised for our iniquities, the chastisement of our peace was upon him, and with his stripes we are healed. KJV

1 Peter 2:24 who is own self bare our sins in his own body on the tree that we being dead to sins, should live unto righteousness by whose stripes ye were healed. KJV

Healing is the children's bread.

The Power of God

Street Meetings: The Making of a Church

In the early nineteen sixties, I learned about street meetings. There was one pastor that went into the neighborhoods having Church services and revivals in people's front yard and on their porches. This pastor's name was Elder T.O. Adams Sr. He would bring his family and other church members with him, and they would have real church services. They read scriptures, have prayer, and sing songs of praise. They would praise the lord clapping their hands playing their tambourines and other musical instruments. They were speaking in unknown tongues and were filled with the Holy Spirit some would fall down in the yard under the influence and power of God. There was no grass in the yards. When the people fell, they would be covered in dust. The people were living in old fashioned shotgun houses that was close together some neighbors, friends and persons walking or passing through would stop and join in The Church Services. Elder Adams would preach working out his church in Clarksdale. He was a sanctified preacher. His lovely wife Mrs. Vernice Adams along with other family members worked tirelessly by his side, also other church members. He named his Church Bradley Temple Church of God in Christ. It was first located on Twelfth Street and relocated to Dr. Martin L. King Drive.

After the pastor would preach, he would make the altar call and different ones would come up to be saved and accept Jesus Christ as their savior. Then the praises would begin all over again. They would rejoice, praise the Lord and dance, clap their hands, and fall out. I had not seen any church services like that before. They would give their testimonies of what the lord had done healed their bodies and saved their souls.

The Adams family would fast a lot. People came to the

church. It was filled to capacity. Sometimes you could hardly find a seat. The family was anointed and also gifted. The mantle fell on them. There were singers, musicians, choir directors and ministers. Mrs. Adams was a Jewel, always working. She went home to be with the Lord first. Then Elder Adams departed this life.

The Doors of the church are still open now. One of his sons Elder T.O. Adams, Jr. is the Pastor. I encourage the Adams family and The Bradley Temple Church Family to continue their walk with the Lord.

Behold, I stand at the door, and knock: if any man hear my voice, and open the door, I will come in to him, and will sup with him, and he with me. Revelations 3:20

The Ones Who Made a Difference

Sister Georgia Ryan

Mother Georgia Ryan was the first church member I met after I had gotten saved. She was the first member to invite us to her house.

Mother Ryan lived alone in a small apartment next to the church. There was a swing on the porch. Her nephew is a member of the church also. When we visited her, she would invite us in. Sometimes she would sit with us on the porch in the swing. She talked about the bible and prayer. Also, how to be saved. How to stay saved and sanctified.

After a visit on the porch, she would invite us inside to pray. We always prayed on our knees. She would begin praying then we would pray with her. Mother Ryan was a true saint of God. Full of compassion and love a humble person a prayer warrior.

My children and I really enjoyed visiting her. She taught us how to pray and what to say. Mother Ryan moved from that apartment. It was remodeled and changed into a fellowship center. We never knew when or where she moved to. All we knew is that we missed her. She went home to be with the Lord in 1977.

The Power of God

Mother Ruby Paden

Mother Ruby Paden a church mother and true saint of God, intercessor, humble, full of compassion, a soul winner, and a witness for the Lord. Full of love a bible scholar and teacher. She was the wife of a pastor, a mother, grandmother, and she loved God and his people. She would teach you how to be saved, and how to stay saved. She taught sanctification and how to receive the baptism in the Holy Ghost. Mother Paden would call, and say come to my house, and I would stop everything and go right over and help her in whatever she was doing.

She would have bible class. We would read the Bible, run references looking up scriptures on different subject matters. I really did enjoy reading and studying the Bible with Mother Paden. She helped me understand the word of God more and I appreciated that she taught the importance of being filled with the Holy Ghost. The Holy Ghost is the power of God. If you don't have the Holy Ghost or Holy Spirit, you have no power. I learned how to fast effectively. Fast days were Tuesday and Friday. My children would fast also beginning Monday night at midnight until three on Tuesday. no food, no water, no medicine. We would consecrate ourselves.

Focus on spiritual things like reading the Bible, prayer, absence of TV or recreational activities. Singing praises and worship songs. If you were married, you agree with your spouse to fast and be celibate until the fast is over then come together in agreement. Sometimes our pastor would ask the church to fast for three days and nights. It disciplines you when you fast. You increase in strength your stomach can shrink and when you come off the fast, we would eat soup and drink juice with some crackers. This is what Mother Paden did teaching others both young and old, until she was unable to do so. She went home to be with the Lord.

The Power of God

Missionary Cherry Scott

Sister Scott was a Sunday School teacher and teacher of life's lessons and how to live.

Once the Lord spoke to me and said seven years. I didn't know the meaning of that. I just listened I didn't know what to say. When I attended church that Sunday and told my pastor's wife. She said seven years means complete.

Once she said I needed to learn how to give. I never told her anything about my giving. I had reservations about giving money to a man. I just didn't want anyone to beat me out of my money. I just said no. I felt like a man should have his own money.

Shortly after that, I was at the post office going up the steps while a man was coming down. He asked me for a certain amount of money. I just said, "no." He was a stranger, never saw him before. I made a few steps away from him and looked back, but he was not there. All his clothing were purple, shirt, pants and shoes. I believed that was an angel. I thought about what sister Scott had said. I felt bad because I did not help him. I had the money he asked for, but I didn't give it to him. That's when I changed my mind about giving. There are times our brothers need help too.

Hebrew 13:1-2 let brotherly love continue. Be not forgetful to entertain strangers for thereby some have entertained angels unawares. KJV

Luke 6:38 Give and it shall be given unto you good measure, pressed down, and shaken together and running over. Shall men give into your bosom for the same measure that ye mete, with all it shall be measured to you again. KJV

The Power of God

Holiness Is Right: My Next Miracle

My mother told me about holiness. She said it was a better way to live. My family moved up North. My mom joined the church of God. That's when her life led her into holiness.

We came from the Baptist Church. We didn't know about paying tithe, fasting, shut in's or anything like that. I watched her how she lived her new life. How she changed. There was a difference in the places she used to go, and the things she did and spoke. She was paying her tithe, fasting and prayer was a new part of her life. She convinced me to get sanctified and said you will love it. I came to Saint James Temple and brought my four daughters with me.

The Pastor, Bishop Scott made the Altar call, and we all went to the altar to get saved. He took us into the church. We were later baptized and accepted into the church and began attending Sunday School, choir rehearsal and prayer and bible study. There were so many bands like sunshine band and purity class for the children to get in. There were so much going on in church it was hardly time for anything else except school, work, and church. It was a wonderful experience like no other we had ever known. Monday night it was purity class and sunshine band. Tuesday night prayer and bible band. Wednesday night choir rehearsal. Friday night Church and tarry service. On Sunday of course Sunday School and church service. Sunday evening YPWW-Young People Willing Workers and Sunshine Band. There was so much going on there was hardly time for anything else. We loved it and was committed to our new life in Christ Jesus.

Being saved from my sins was a miracle what a beautiful life to live. My children loved it too!

Filled with The Holy Ghost: My Third Miracle

May 31st. 1981 on a Saturday night the Lord filled me with the Holy Ghost. I had worked so hard that day. The patient load was heavy at the hospital. I managed to get off at three fifteen and went home. A church member called and said There was a one-night revival going on at Rehoboth, did I want to go? I said yes. I had been fasting and seeking the lord for the Baptism in the Holy Ghost. I told the Lord to fill me with the Holy Ghost or else I will fast until I die. I was serious with God. I had been seeking the Holy Ghost for five years. I was tired of myself I really was too tired to go anywhere, but I went to church that night.

Rehoboth was located on Florida Street Pastored by Elder David Taylor. Elder Albert Pass was the Evangelist and pastor of Christ Temple Church of God in Christ in Holly Springs, Mississippi.

I went to the Church that night and it was very crowded and hard to find a vacant pew. When I arrived at Church praise and testimony services were in progress. The Church members were singing and praising and dancing clapping their hands, just rejoicing in the Lord. When the praise and testimony services were over then the Evangelist began to preach the message. I don't remember what he preached about that night but after the message he made the Altar call.

Many persons came before the altar. Elder Pass began to pray for the ones that came. Many were blessed and some were filled with the Holy Ghost. It was such an awesome night. It seems that everyone was blessed. I know I was the lord filled me that night. That was the best thing that happened to me. I was so full I could not stop speaking in unknown tongues. When I tried to talk to the Church members no words were coming out. Only the heavenly language. So, I went home, and I don't remember when I went to bed that night. I was so full of the Holy Ghost. I didn't want to stop. I kept going on and, on my family, just didn't know what to do. Oh, how wonderful, how glorious.

It was a Pentecost night.

Acts 2:1-4 And when the day of Pentecost was fully come, they were all with one accord in one place. And suddenly there came a sound from heaven as a rushing mighty wind, and it filled all the house where they were sitting. And there appeared unto them cloven tongues like as of fire and it sat upon each of them. And they were all filled with the Holy Ghost, and began to speak with other tongues as the spirit gave them utterance KJV

The Churches need to get back to fasting, prayer, shut-ins and seeking the face of God. Seek God's will. We need the power of God working through us and for us like never before. The church has been asleep too long. And needs to wake up and be about our father's business.

No More Business as Usual

Seek the will of God. Seek his face fast, pray. Spend time with God. Read his word. Meditate on it. Ask for more wisdom and knowledge and discernment. Ask the Lord for more faith. Faith comes by hearing and hearing by the word of God. Ask the Lord for that mountain moving faith.

Mother Artelia Shannon Kelly

This is the testimony of Mother Artelia Shannon Kelly a missionary and welfare worker that visited homes where children lived.

There was a certain day she visited a family in the county just outside the city not knowing that an inmate had escaped from the Mississippi Department of Corrections at Parchmen. That person was armed and considered extremely dangerous. It just happened that he came to the home where she was.

He overpowered the people that were there, tied them up and put them in a room and left.

Mother Kelly said being tied up did not stop her from praying. She kept on praying until someone came, found them tied up and released them, the same day. They thanked God no lives were lost. They all had a testimony to tell.

Mother Kelly told this testimony over and over again. She said this in Church. The lord will deliver you in time of troubles. Just call on Jesus, He will answer prayer. She lived many years after being held hostage and thanked the Lord how he spared their lives. That escapee did not harm anyone. Prayer works.

Revelation 12:11 And they overcame him by the blood of the lamb and by the word of their testimony. KJV

We are overcomers through Christ Jesus

What A Miracle!

Brother Will Womack

Testimony of Brother Will Womack a deacon at the church, a praying saint of God. A humble man that liked to sing praise and worship songs during testimonial services. One of his songs were--

John saw a number, way in the middle of the air. John saw a number, way in the middle of the air.

When he sang, everyone would join in singing and praising the Lord, clapping their hands, shouting, and dancing, and the lifting up of hands, calling on Jesus. Sometimes when my daughters and I get together now, we sang the praise songs he used to sing.

Brother and Sister Womack were two humble and beautiful people. They lived by the Sunflower River on Sunflower Avenue. They would plant vegetable gardens with a lot of vegetables. They would just give them away to many people. Deacon Womack had another hobby. He liked to fish as well and gave fish away.

He had an old wooden boat that he would take to the lake with his fishing tackle. One day he went fishing and launched his boat out in the water. That day something happened. His boat fell apart. He lost his tackle, and he could not swim. So, he sank to the bottom of the lake and held his breath and walked out on dry land He Lived to tell his testimony again and again how the lord spared his life.

There was another song the deacon loved to sing. *He laid the foundation and made the way plain, what more can Jesus do. What more can Jesus do?* The lord preserved Deacon Womack's life as he preserved Jonah's life in the fish's belly. Remembering the life and legacy of the older saints how they propelled us on their shoulders. God still works Miracles.

Mother Lula Meeks

A humble servant just being there, loving, and caring, giving words of encouragement, full of compassion. She was a sanctified mother full of the Holy Ghost.

Mother Meeks would prepare the Holy Communion along with other Mothers and covered the elements, until served. After Bishop Scott would bring the message, the entire Church would sing songs like this, *I know it was the blood, I know it was the blood, I know it was the blood for me. One day when I was lost, he died upon the cross. I know it was the blood for me.*

Three of Mother Meek's sons are Ministers. The mantle fell on them. God knows who he can trust. After our pastor Bishop Scott would bring the message on communion day, He would have someone read a scripture like this

1 Corinthians 11:23-26

23. For I have received of the Lord that which also I delivered unto you that the Lord Jesus the same night in which he was betrayed took bread.

24. And when he had given thanks, he break it, and said take, eat, this is my body which is broken for you. This do in remembrance of me.

25. For as often as ye eat this bread and drink this cup, ye do shew the lord's death til he come.KJV

Mother Nellie Chambers

Mother Nellie Chambers was a humble servant and saint of God. The president of prayer and Bible Band. Bible study was every Tuesday Night. She would open with song, scripture, and prayer. Then the study of the lesson. Mother was a great teacher. My Children and I loved going to prayer and bible study. Even though it was held on school nights. We all attended. Mother Chambers was a prayer warrior, she was an inspiration to us. My children learned the bible and were grateful in doing so. She encouraged us to pray.

We would pray on our knees and study the word together.

Mother Pearl Allen

Mother Pearl Allen- had a special praise song she would sing, and the congregation would join in and sing.

> What I am,
>
> What I am,
>
> Jesus made me,
>
> what I am
>
> what I am,
>
> Jesus made me what I am
>
> Saints,
>
> what I am,
>
> what I am
>
> Jesus made me what I am.

After Mother Allen would sing, rejoice, and praise the Lord. The church would sing and praise the Lord with her. Speaking in tongues and dancing.

Sunday School

We have always been blessed with great Sunday School Instructors at Saint James Temple. The first one was Mrs. Gussie Riley, a meek and humble servant, Bible scholar and teacher. Soft spoken and explain the lessons where anyone could understand.

The next was Mother Riley's daughter Sister Laura Adams who is an educator and bible scholar also teaching life's lessons on how to live.

Our pastor's wife sister Cherry Scott another bible instructor teaching life's lessons. They all made an impact in my life. They made a difference to a lot of ladies. I thank God for all of them. Sisters Riley, Gooden, and Scott has gone home to be with the Lord. Sister Adams is still teaching the bible and explaining the word.

Sunday School Day was an annual event to be remembered. We looked forward to it every year. It was always an exciting day to me.

On that day you did not know who your teacher would be. They would exchange classes. And we would give special offerings. Sunday School is the largest bible study group in the church. There are more church members involved in Sunday School than any other Bible study group in the church.

2 Tim. 2:15 Study to show thyself approved unto God, a workman that needeth not to be ashamed, rightly dividing the word of truth. KJV

Everyone should attend Sunday School. You need Sunday School and Sunday school needs you.

Mrs. Pollye Walker

Mrs. Pollye Walker was a saint of God. Filled with the Holy Ghost. A gospel singer. A leader in the adult choir at Saint James Temple Cogic. She was a soloist and sang soprano. She led many songs under the anointing of the Holy Ghost. One song she used to sing was *I found Jesus and I'm glad*. Some of the songs she used to sing are being sung by some of her family members now. Sister Walker went home to be with the lord. Her untimely death was a shocking experience to all that knew her and left a void in our lives. I saw her once in a vision out in a soybean field. The beans were ready for harvest, and she had a message to deliver. Signs and wonders.

Mrs. Larrenia Moore

Song writer, soloist and Gospel Singer Mrs. Larrenia Moore, my mother wrote gospel songs, sang solos, and would sing at revivals, funerals, and church services. Mother would write song after song and made a song book to keep them in. She sewed the book with needle and thread and put her songs into it and kept them together. None of her songs were ever recorded or put to music. She could sing in different keys, soprano, alto, tenor, and bass. She knew how to sing parts. She would call us together and say, "Come on you all, talking to us, her children and let's sing these songs."

Sometimes holding the baby in one arm and the song book in the other hand. We would gather around her; she would tell us the words to the songs and how to sing them. We would sing those songs together.

Mother was singing during the late nineteenth forties and through the nineteen fifties.

During that time a pastor would come from Memphis, Tennessee named The Reverend Jasper Williams Sr. Running Revivals throughout The Mississippi Delta. He pastored a church in the city of Memphis

There was a Church at Jonestown Mississippi pastored by The Rev. Edgar Jude named Saint Luke Missionary Baptist Church. At the time of Revival, the word would spread everywhere. My mother would sign solos before he brought the message.

The Churches were the pillars of the communities. At revival time, my father was a deacon named Warren Moore. He would get off work and go to the Church early and open the doors and began praying. We would go to church with him riding on back of the truck.

At the Church there would be families waiting outside. My father would open by singing and praying. So many people would come to church from miles around. Some walking others riding, adults and children. If you wanted a seat, you came early because the church filled up. Chairs were put in the aisles and around the choir and wherever a chair could be placed. Children were sitting on the floor. When the church filled up, they would open the windows so the ones outside could hear. Some sat in their cars, and trucks. Some did bring their own chairs and sat in the yard. There would probably be a thousand people at any revival. The people would sing and pray, shout, and praise the lord. Men and women would be shouting It was old fashioned church at its best. Sometimes the revival would go on two to three weeks. It was talked about for a long time. An event to remember.

We the people need to return to worship God with all our strength. Sometimes services would last a long time. We need to spend time with God.

One of our siblings had a love for rice, and when she wanted rice, she wanted it no matter where we were. She would tell us; I want some rice starting out quietly and get louder. She would continue until we could no longer ignore her. Sometimes we had to leave church before the benediction, so we started bringing rice with us for her. It not she would have a complete meltdown.

The bible says forsaken not the assembly of yourselves together as the manner as some is.

Mrs. Everlena Christian

Teacher or Morals

Mrs. Everlena Christian had an impact on many young lady's lives. She was full of love and compassion, and always generous, gave good instructions. She was a Christian woman that started a group of young women meeting at her house. She taught good morals. Sometimes there would be from six to ten. Mrs. Christian was a leader in the neighborhood and full of wisdom, gave good instructions. She would tell us to take our children to church and teach them what's right.

She was an entrepreneur that had a flower shop built onto her home on Jefferson Street. She made and sold flowers from her business and had them delivered to their destinations.

Earlier in her life she developed a broken hip and never had surgery for it. She walked with a limp, never used a cane, it did not stop her from doing anything, she wanted to do. She was always dressed well and had integrity. She walked wherever she wanted to go. Mrs. Christian has helped many people. There need to be more people like her. She had a husband and one son.

When we came together as a group. She would serve refreshments and we always had devotion and benediction.

Part Two

Dreams and Visions

For a dream cometh through the multitude of business. Ecclessiates.5:3A KJV

Sometimes we have dreams because of some kind of food we have eaten.

For the vision is yet for an appointed time, at the end it shall speak and not lie. Though it tarry wait for it because it will surely come. It will not tarry. Habakuk 3

Where there is no vision the people perish.

Leaders are visionaries. The absence of vision causes people to perish. The presence of vison brings hope and change.

He that keepteh the law; happy is he. Psalm 29:18 First, visions must be written. Second it must be clear to be understood. Third it must be motivating to those who read and receive with patience. The visions are for an appointed time. It is sure to come. Resources follow visions. *But the just shall live by faith; Habakkuk 2:46*

And it shall come to pass afterward, that I will pour out my spirit upon all flesh; and your sons and your daughters shall prophesy, your old men shall dream dreams, your young men shall see visions: Joel 2:28

Once I had a vision of a whirlwind. It was so beautiful blue as the sky. They were some very large shoes over in it. There was an individual standing by, and they just stepped over into the huge shoes. They will fill some large shoes. Then the vision was over. Vision in Hebrew means the divine revelation of the truth.

My First Vision

After the Lord told me seven years, I began to have visions and dreams. I don't know what exactly my gifts are, but I have some, more than one.

In this vision I saw ice all over the highway. It was summer and the temperature was above a hundred every day. So, a few days after seeing that it became a reality.

On highway 61 South of Clarksdale a semi was traveling and overturned and spilled its cargo. It had a load of fish that was on ice. This happened near the town of Bobo. At the same time Bobo was having water crisis. They had no water. Their well was broken. The people began gathering fish an ice. The fish for eating and the ice was saved to use for water for flushing out their drains.

My Next Vision

This vision was about church members drowning in the pews. I saw young and old sitting in their seats and water was rising, first around their legs. Then it came up to their waist, the water kept on rising up around the chest an up to their necks. I could only see the heads were just above the water. I didn't know the meaning of this. I told my pastor about the vision. Maybe the Lord will reveal it to him, or maybe he knew already. Bishop Scott listened attentively.

Signs and Wonders

One Sunday when praise and testimonial service were in progress. I was standing at my seat singing and clapping my hands and praising the Lord. Suddenly I was turned upside down. My head was on the floor where my feet were supposed to be. I could not stop what happened to me. I had no control over that. My body was as stiff as a board. My shoulders and chest were wedged between the seats. The ladies came to my rescue and helped me. Some men came also and moved me from between the pews. I was unable to speak could not move at my own will. I don't know how long it lasted.

I was like an 8 x 16 what the carpenters use for building. I knew what was happening to me, but I didn't know why or how this happened. I knew it was the spirit of God. The Holy Spirit does what he wants to do and to whom he wants to. I believe it happened to make a believer out of someone.

Signs and wonders are found throughout the Bible. It is the power of God.

I told my prayer partner about it, and she said the same thing happened to her mother while attending the convocation in Memphis, before it was moved to St. Louis. My prayer partner's name was Doshie Pigee, and her mother was Mrs. Renner Bell Pigee.

I heard of this happening to another person who was a man. He was at a dollar store and the Holy Spirit Spoke to him and said, go into the store and stand on your head. He entered the store and stood on his head. He obeyed the spirit of God. Another sign and wonder. They are throughout the Bible.

Remember Moses and the burning bush at the mountain.

Angels in The House

I made my house a house of worship and a house of prayer.

One day I was praying in my living room, and I was on my knees for a while. I just looked up and that's when I saw angels all around the room. I didn't know what to do or say so I just kept on praying. After a while I looked up again and there were more angels standing shoulder to shoulder in the hallway. I still didn't know what to say or do. So, I kept on praying. And after a while I looked up again and they were all gone. So, I ended my prayer. I had just had an angelic visitation.

Angels are God's ministering spirits. I thank God for angels.

Beheading Demons

One Wednesday Our pastor called the church members and said to meet him at church for prayer at nine. About six members came to pray. We arrived on time and entered the sanctuary. The pastor led the prayer services.

After praying for about one hour, I had a vision, and I told it to the pastor. I saw myself at the front door and as the people came into the church there was a hole in the floor just outside the door and demons were coming up out of the hole trying to leap onto the people as they entered. I was standing at the door with a sword in my hands and as the demons came up out of the hole, I was beheading them with that sword in prayer.

Home Coming

I was at home one day and I felt that someone needed my help. I asked other friends to go with me, but everyone was too busy. So, I went alone.

I went to Memphis, Tenn., to visit some parks. My first stop was the army and navy parks on second street. I saw several homeless people there. I ministered to them. Then I went to the park on Riverside Drive. I didn't know the name of it then, But I later learned that it was the Tom Lee Park. I saw people asleep on park benches. It was summer, the weather was nice, sun shining. I was walking across the park where a lady was sleeping. I kept on walking toward her. When I got close to her, I could see that she was covered with spiders. So, I rushed to her to wake her up. I was calling out, "Lady, Lady, wake up!"

Did you know you are covered with spiders? She said no. So, I began helping her to remove them. They were all over clothing and in her hair just everywhere. It seemed like she was sleeping so well, I didn't want to wake her until I came close enough to see the spiders. When we finished removing them, we began to talk and fellowship. We introduced ourselves. She said she was homeless and, in the past, had been saved and was a member of the Church of God in Christ. She had lost everything she had nothing. No house or car. She had a few things in a shopping cart and the clothing she was wearing. She also lost her job.

I offered to help this lady, but she refused my help. I offered to take or send her to the beauty shop, she refused that also. I asked about the church she used to attend. The pastor had passed away. There was a new pastor, they had a new leader that she did not know. I instructed her to go return to God and the Church and talk to the new pastor and tell him who she was and to go back home.

The reason she refused help from me because she had a lot of money. She pulled out a large sum of it. She said she could not accept any from me. I told her put it away before someone else sees it and try to rob you. I ministered to her and encouraged her to return to her church. She promised me she would do that and go to the beauty shop. I visited the park several times after that. I never saw her again. Coming home, coming home

Jeremiah 3:14-15 Turn o backsliding children, saith the Lord; for I am married unto you; and I will take you one of a cities and two of a family and I will bring you to Zion. And I will give you pastors according to mine heart, which shall feed you with knowledge and understanding.

My First Vision of an Infant

One day I was at home, and I had a vision of an infant. Someone left the child at my front door. It was a very young infant wrapped in a light green blanket. It was wet with dew. I came from the back of the house up to the front I looked out the side window and saw the child I rushed outside to get the baby and brought her in the house at once.

I observed when I unwrapped her. She was a girl, a very beautiful fair skinned. She was quiet, not in distress or crying.

I immediately called the police Department and reported it. Then the vision was over.

A Vision of Water Underground

I had a vision of water under the ground in a park across the street from one of my daughter's houses. It was an underground stream. Then it became a reality. I thought it was a fishpond that had been covered. The park already had a gazebo, some park benches, a walking trail, and climbing bars for the children to exercise on. But no water. Only portable latrines. The Blue Cross Blue Shield Inc. decided to turn it into a water park that's where the water came from, and they added more items for the children's recreation. I told my church members and my family about the vision I had about the park we watched the park come to fruition as a water park.

Fire Burning Underneath My Feet

One Tuesday in 2018, I had attended prayer and bible band. After I prayed the prayer of dismissal, and we were about to leave the church.

I saw smoke coming up through the floor. Then it came up around our feet, then around our waist and it kept on coming up higher around our heads. Then I told the prayer group what I had seen. I saw fire underneath the floor burning, but the fire never came above the floor.

I don't know how to interpret visions or dreams. They are signs and wonders in the earth. To God be the glory for the things he has done.

The Voice of The Lord

The Lord spoke to me one day and said, your two sons will be ministers.

Well, I didn't know what to do or say. Because I don't have any sons, so I just listened. I didn't say anything. I just didn't know what to do. I never told anyone about that, I just kept that to myself at the time.

A few years passed and I was at my daughter's house when her two sons came walking through the house. The older son came from the hallway crossed through the living room and came into the kitchen. Then her younger son came from the hall and came through the living room into the kitchen.

It was then the Lord said to me, these are the two ministers. That's when I told my daughter what the Lord had said.

The younger son had just had a birthday. I had started teaching him the Lord's Prayer. He didn't know all of the words yet. So, they were having a Christmas program at his pre-school. The teacher asks his class did anyone know the Lord's Prayer. He said yes, and they put him on the program to do or say the prayer. He said it as best as he could only missing a few words. He was three turning four. He had not learned to read yet.

I told the older son to read a chapter per day in his Bible. I didn't know what to do. I told the Lord to bring it to pass in his own timing. I thank God that he looked down into my family to see someone he can trust. I say, "Oh Lord brings it to pass in Jesus' name."

The Spirit of God Flowing Like a River

When the lord told me seven years. I began seeing things in the spirit. I've had some dreams, but I have more visions. You must know the real dreams because the others don't add up to reality. Sometimes you dream when you have eaten different kinds of food and you will know when it's not real.

I saw the spirit of God flowing like a river. It was about one foot above the ground. It moved closer toward me and kept on coming. It met me head on and came upon my abdomen entered into it and then came out of my mouth and it kept on flowing just like a river. Then the vision was over.

John 7:38 He that believeth on me as the scripture hath said, out of his belly shall flow rivers of living water. KJV

Miracles of The Century

On September 7, 1918, my mother was birthed into this world during the pandemic called the Spanish flu. It took the lives of so many people during World War one, worldwide. Many soldiers lost their lives and possibly half a billion people were infected.

Anthony and Roxie Gholston, my grandparents had 5 children; my mother was the 6th born during that outbreak of the Pandemic.

They received a miracle from God. My grandmother and mother were spared and did not Catch that virus. Not only them the whole family was spared. Oh, what a mighty Miracle was wrought. All of the children three boys, Nathaniel, Joe Samuel, and Emanuel, and three girls, Ira Leona, Asalene, and my mother Larrenia, did not catch that virus, nor did my grandfather. No illness or loss of life in this family.

God is still working miracles today. Another pandemic in 2019 until now, Covid 19, still no serious illness or loss of life in this family. Many people are dying all around us even until now. Some friends, neighbors, pastors and pastors' wives, church members and so many more that we do not know. But we thank God for sparing our lives. Nothing but miracles. To God be the glory for the things he has done. He said in his word, *I AM God and I change not. Malachi 3:6 Jesus Christ the same yesterday and today and forever. Heb.13:8 KJV*

God is still working miracles today.

A Double Family Miracle

In 2009 I began fasting for thirty days not knowing what or why I was going on that fast. I didn't know what was about to happen. I had a hunger for fasting. I would bring a church mother to church with me sometimes. So, One Sunday, I gave her a ride and she asked me, "what was I fasting for?" I didn't answer her. I could not, knowing myself why. I never told her I was fasting. I guess she just knew or figured it out. That fast was for thirty days only, but I was not satisfied. So, I waited for a while and went on a forty day fast, a few months later. When I ended the second fast, I was satisfied. Still not knowing why.

Later that year one of my daughters came to me with a report from her physician having been diagnosed with cancer. She was crying not knowing what to do. She was devastated. I talked to her and told her not to cry because she is not going to die but live. I spoke life into her. and she will live and raise her children she stopped crying and listened to what I was telling her. We went home. Her doctor scheduled her for surgery. The procedure went well.

I prayed for her. After surgery she had chemotherapy and later returned to her working schedule. She has done well. Today she is cancer free and no medical setbacks, even after radiation. Months later, another daughter received a depressing report but did not inform me. I heard her husband tell her; you need to tell your mother what your physician told you. She didn't tell me right away, but later, so we began making arrangements for treatment and surgery. They chose a surgeon and made an appointment. Her surgery was successful. Then chemotherapy and radiation. Now she is cancer free. God is a healer, and healing is the children's bread.

Isaiah 53:4-5 surely, he hath borne our griefs and carried our sorrows: yet we did esteem him stricken, smitten of God and afflicted. But he was wounded for our transgressions, he was bruised for our iniquities: the chastisements of our peace was upon him: and with his stripes we are healed. KJV

1 Peter 2:24 Who his own self bare our sins in his own body on the tree, that we being dead to sin, should live unto righteousness by whose stripes ye were healed. KJV

Both of my daughters remain healed until this day. Believe God and be healed, be delivered, and be set free. To God be the Glory for the things He has done.

A Miracle in Alligator Mississippi

Growing up in the country, Bolivar County with parents and an older brother, there was a lake there called Alligator Lake. It has been said that the town got its name because there were alligators in the lake.

My father always worked on Saturdays. My mom was a housewife. We attended church on Sundays. We went to town on Saturdays. We would sometimes walk on the sidewalk or sit on the park benches in front of the stores eating Ice Cream cones, candy, and other snacks, with our mother at our side. Our dad would work at some of the stores, everyone knew who he was.

That day we were sitting on a bench in front of a store and someone driving a car was trying to park and lost control and ran over us. My mother was able to get us out of the way but not herself. So, the car ran over her. We could see her under the car, her arms, and legs. We were crying, I was three and my brother was six.

Someone went to get our father and he came. Some people helped to get the car off her and picked her up, took her down the street to the doctor's office that doctor was Dr. Pierce and we went with our dad to the office still crying. That was awful to see our mother get run over by a car. When she came out, she had a large wrap around her head and a long white wrap on one leg I think it was a cast. We went home at last. I was glad to see our mother at home. We found out she had a head wound and a broken leg.

The town Marshall came, and I don't know what happen to that person. That was a miracle that she lived. I thank God for miracles. To God be the Glory to the things He has done.

A Miracle Baby

A young lady was attending church one Sunday had a special request. She wanted the Lord to bless her with a child.

After the pastor finished the message and made the Altar Call this lady came to the Altar and informed the pastor of her request. Elder Albert Pass instructed her mother to place her hand on the lady's abdomen, then he placed his hand on hers and began to pray the prayer of faith. The lord blessed her with a baby girl. I know, that was my daughter and granddaughter. She is a healthy child. The Lord blessed us with a miracle. Thank God for miracles.

The Explosion of the Red Panther in Clarksdale

The night the chemical plant exploded was very frightening. In our hometown, late one night we were all asleep in bed and the phone rang. Someone called to wake us up. One of the girls went to answer the phone but she was a sleepy head and did not get the message clearly. She went back to bed after answering the phone. So, we continued to sleep. She didn't tell the family.

After some time lapsed, someone called again to awaken us, another family member answered this time that person was screaming on the phone saying get out, leave, the chemical plant has blown up. Come on out of the house. We rushed and put on clothed, got in the car and left the house.

Once we were outside it was hard to breathe there was so much fog we could hardly see. The fallout was so great like rain drops we went to the post office which was a fallout shelter. No one was there. Then the city auditorium. No one were there. We didn't see anyone anywhere. I suppose every one left town. Then went out to the stadium which was outside of town. We could breathe better the air was clear.

We just laid out on the bleachers and went to sleep. Other people came to the stadium and rested on the bleachers we remained there most of the day. Our family didn't need emergency care. Thank God we were alright. The fallout was so thick it took the paint off some cars. Another miracle.

The Unexpected

We are living in a time that things are happening that has not happened before in our time. Things has changed, but God has not. He is the same yesterday, today and forever.

It was reported in the news during the time hurricane Ida was wreaking havoc. We know that rivers normally flow downstream. It was stated that the Mississippi river began flowing upstream and did so for four hours. That is not normal. Not only are the waterways changing, animals are changing also.

My pet puppy Sugar was in the backyard and a rabbit came into the yard. They saw each other, they looked and just ignored the other was there. Usually, dogs chase rabbits but that did not happen. They were in the yard more than fifteen or twenty minutes together.

They were quiet, mild mannered and continued what they were doing. Just walking through the grass and looking. No signs of excitement or fear. I watched them the whole time.

People are changing, also with decision making and attitudes. There has been so much sickness and death due to covid 19. Everyone has been affected by it whether it was a loss of a family member or church member, friend, or acquaintance. It has been a lot of hurt and pain. Loss of employment for some or relocation and children sometimes are included in this. They have needs and feelings also. Even some children have lost their lives to the virus. But we can make things a little better when we help one another by caring, giving, and sharing with love.

The Power of God

Part Three

Bishop Timothy Titus Scott

Honoring Bishop Timothy Titus Scott

Special Honor To
Bishop Timothy Titus Scott
The Longest Reining Bishop
In The Church of God in Christ
Since January 1973 until
April 2020

On December 18, 1931, Timothy Titus Scott was born to Elder Matthew and Melissa Scott in East Chicago Indiana. He was one of ten children. He was saved at the age of eight. He received his Bachelor of Science Degree from Mississippi Valley State College at Itta Bena, Miss. After receiving his education, he was drafted into the military and served his country from 1952 until 1954.

Bishop Scott carried on the ministry of Jesus Christ wearing the prophetic mantle of responsibility and God's accompanying power. These garments have been worn from the Exodus until the present time by special people. The power of God is the strongest force in the Universe. Bishop Scott was saved at an early age.

He Was One That Made a Difference in Our Lives. Our beloved Pastor and Bishop Timothy Titus Scott made his transition to be with the Lord on April 3, 2020. He was loved and missed by many who knew him. His untimely death left a void in our lives. He was appointed Pastor of St. James Temple COGIC and consecrated as Bishop of the Northern Mississippi Jurisdiction by the Presiding Bishop J.O. Patterson, Sr, and the General Board of the Church of God in Christ in January 1973, at Dr. Martin Luther King Blvd. He met Ms. Cherry Mae Mitchell and they were united in Holy Matrimony on June 3,1956.

The Lord blessed this union with ten wonderful children, six sons and four daughters. Five of the sons are ministers. One has gone home to be with the Lord. Bishop Scott was a leader, pastor, teacher, husband, father, grandfather, a builder of families and buildings. He was a humble man and servant of God.

The Church expanded under his great leadership. Additional ministries were added. The missions and the food pantry and clothes closet to help people in the neighborhood and surrounding areas. The mission is located on Sunflower and Martin Luther King BLVD. The Family Life Center is an expansion to the local church in the rear with more parking spaces added. The state Temple was erected with office buildings added with rooms for lodging when meetings are being held and more parking spaces added at 376 Sunflower Avenue. Then The Heritage Building was erected on Sunflower Avenue across the street from the state Temple and named in Bishop Scott's honor.

Bishop Scott has ordained many ministers, Elders, appointed pastors to churches, added more Districts appointed more superintendents and made many other appointments when and wherever they were needed in the churches and state. Bishop Scott worked tirelessly many years for the Lord and encouraged others. He was a witness, soul winner and servant for the Lord along with his wife Mrs. Cherry Scott.

The Mantle fell in his own house and in the church upon his children and other church members. There were ministers, musicians, singers, choir directors, teachers, Authors, song writers, poets or poem writers and the gifts keep flowing. More educator's Bishop Scott has touched many lives and the blessings keeps on flowing. At one time there were so many ministers at church, young teenagers, and older ones too.

Psalm 41:1-2 *Blessed is he that considereth the poor: The lord will deliver him in time of trouble. The Lord will preserve him and keep him alive: and he shall be blessed upon the earth: and thou wilt not deliver him unto the will of his enemies. KJV*

He was a servant of the almighty God. A builder working with his hands doing carpentry work. One hot summer day he was at his apartments downtown the Malissa Garden, named after his mother, it was very hot that entire week. The temperatures were in the triple digits, above 100. That day the temperature was one hundred and three.

I was taking care of business on that day over town, and just happened to drive by and see him outside working in that intense heat without a head covering. I didn't stop or say anything to him. I didn't have a cell phone they may not have been invented yet. So, I drove home and used my phone to call my pastor's house. One of the son's answered. I told him I saw Bishop Scott out in the Sun working with nothing on his head, at the apartments.

I told him to go and get him out of the Sun. And reminded him the temperature was one hundred and three, that very day. The son said we know he is working at the apartments. That is what he does. I said but it is too hot go and get him out of the sun. He said what am I going to do or say to him? I said I don't know what you are going to say but go get him. They got him out of the sun and took him home. He was alright. I never heard anything different. Thank God for his children, following up on that, and taking care of the man of God.

Bishop Timothy Titus Scott was a caring person. Always helping other people. He was a humble man. I remember the time when the state of Mississippi passed a law concerning patients in mental institutions. If the person were able to say they wanted to go home, they released them from the hospital. My mother had a cousin that was in a south Mississippi hospital, and he was able to say he wanted to leave. James Robinson graduated from high school and served in the military as a marine. He was a leather neck and a sharpshooter. As time went by, he lost his mind and had to be treated in a mental institution.

At the time of his release, they didn't inform the family at all. They just let him go. When he called me, he was already at the Greyhound Bus station with his ticket in his hand. I answered the phone. He said I am out of the hospital and I'm coming to live with you. I tried to convince him to go and live with his sister Mary who lived in Louisville, Mississippi. He was closer to where she was. I could not talk him out of coming to my house. He said I am coming to live with you. I want to live with you.

At that time, the situation at my house was a small three bedroom with one bath. My husband was ill and not able to work. My mother had gotten ill up north and was not able to work. She came to live with us. We had four teenage daughters in school. It was hard to get in the bathroom. At that moment I didn't know what to do. I went into the utility room and cried. I was taking care of sick people all day on the job having to come home and care for my family members it was overwhelming. It was too much.

I asked the Lord why am I having to do this? It was too much at the time. The lord spoke to me and said," you are going to live to be a hundred." I stopped crying and came out. I still had to find a place for James to live. There were seven already in the house. The New Year had just come in. There was a blizzard, it had snowed, and ice was everywhere. The roads and trees were frozen over.

I thought about Bishop Scott my pastor. I called him and told him about the situation. There were some apartments behind the church on Fourth Street. They were to house the church members coming from out of town when they came to the meetings. I asked him could James stay there until I find him a place. He said Yes.

He reminded me that was just temporary because the next meeting was the first week in March. I thanked him and he gave me a key. When James arrived. I picked him up. He came to the house and visited for a while. Then I took him to the room behind the Church.

Oh, what a miracle that was. I was relieved at last. So, I began looking downtown for a room for James. It was hard. The weather was cold and bad. There were no vacant rooms available. I kept on looking. Just before the month of March came in. I found a room upstairs and rented it. Just in time before the meeting. I told James about the room. He didn't understand why he had to move. I had a hard time getting him out and over to his place. At last, that was over. Mary his sister would alternate paying rent every two weeks.

I thanked Bishop Scott for letting James stay in the apartment. I don't know what I would have done without his help. I thanked God. Oh, what a miracle that was.

Bishop Scott and his Wife Cherry Scott

Bishop Dr. T. D. Lockett

Bishop Dr. T.D. Lockett pastor and founder of the Faith Temple Church of God which was established in 1967 in Kalamazoo, Michigan. He is the senior presiding Bishop of the Faith Temple Churches of God Incorporated. The Ecclesiastical Part of his life began in the fall of 1960. As he came to realize his life was not in accordance with God's word. After hearing the word of God, a number of times he received salvation in July of 1961. In the spring of 1967, he had very strong stirrings to build a church for God, and after concern was granted, he began with the missions Faith Temple was then organized in November 1967. And in May 1969 was chartered with the state of Michigan's Department of treasury and registered in Washington, DC as a cooperation and recognized as an independent organization.

Bishop Lockett was selected to hold the position of presiding Bishop and was inaugurated on September 26, 1971. Since his inauguration. God has continued to bless his ministry. In 1999, Bishop Lockett received an Honorary Doctor of Ministry Degree from the ministerial training Institute of Inglewood, California, an International Accredited Bible College. Through the Ministry of Jesus Christ, he has reached thousands via radio, television, and travel and has formed firm friendships, and fellowships locally and abroad.

A high point of his ministry was he twice traveled to Nigeria, West Africa and ministered to over 750,000 people in one service. During both visits he witnessed the poverty and struggles of most of the Natives and the Meager means for day-to-day survival. He returned home and organized a foreign ministry mission called "Africa Now" which raised $20,000 to aid the people in Africa under his leadership, Faith Temple also operates new direction outreach center which furthers his vision of community outreach by providing a variety of programs and services to homeless and hungry youth, adults and families and others less fortunate in the community.

In April 2013, the Lord blessed Faith Temple to acquire property at its current location at 402 South Westnedge Avenue downtown Kalamazoo and the first service was held August 4, 2013. The larger facility offers 46,000 square feet including a full-sized gymnasium which offers great opportunities for future growth and to better serve and minister to the needs of the people in the community. Many churches have comprised the name

"Faith Temple Church of God" through the United States. With great talent and dedication and the power of God Bishop Lockett with his beautiful wife Mrs. Quella and family along with the Church family has worked tirelessly down through the years worshipping and serving God's People. He is a humble servant, full of compassion, a teacher, bible scholar and hospitable, prayer warrior and loves God.

Bishop T D Lockett Ministering Under the Anointing

Since Covid 19, many churches had closed their doors to protect the people and trying to follow protocol for safety. Now they have begun to open and allow church services to be held in the buildings again. Thank God for social media that has kept the congregation together. We need to stay connected and not lose that fellowship with God and each other.

One Sunday Morning on Facebook Bishop Lockett was preaching under the anointing. As he moved, I saw the spirit of God move with him. When he moved to the right, the spirit moved with him as he moved to the left, the spirit moved also and when he stood still, the spirit stood still. It was around him. It was a white cloud.

When the anointing is present it destroys yokes. Bodies are healed sinners are saved. The people are blessed. It releases the bound and sets the captives free.

Isaiah 61:1-3 The spirit of the lord God is upon me: because the lord hath anointed me to preach good tidings unto the meek he hath sent me to bind up the broken hearted to proclaim liberty to the captives and the opening of the prison to them that are bound. To proclaim the acceptable year of the Lord, and the day of vengeance of our God. To comfort all that mourn. KJV.

Another Sunday at Bishop Lockett's Church after the message the spirit of the Lord was present. The people were rejoicing, shouting, dancing and there were some huge white angel wings extending from almost to the top of the building down to almost the floor. God was present in the house.

Bishop T.D. and Mother Quella Lockett celebrated 65 years of marriage on Christmas Eve 2021 the Lord have blessed them with 11 children, 29 grandchildren and currently 11 great grandchildren. They are so bountifully blessed of the Lord.

To God be the glory for the things he has done.

Mother Quella Lockett departed this life on Friday April 29th. Her service was held on Tuesday May 10th at Galilee Church in Kalamazoo Michigan.

About the Author

In August of 1963 after working on the farm as a sharecropper, I relocated to the city of Clarksdale. I attended classes got my high school diploma and began clerical training that included typing, filing, shorthand, bookkeeping, and office etiquette. I was determined to make life better for me and my family. Years later I attended three years of college.

As time passed, I got saved and my spiritual life became alive when I committed my ways to the lord. It was a learning experience. Everything changed the lord wants obedience, humility, commitment with love for him and our fellowman and serving with our whole heart in worship and praise. When you draw near to God, he will draw near unto you. You can't prosper on you own. It's the power of God that prospers you. All blessings comes from him. *Deuteronomy 8:18 It is he that giveth the power to get wealth, that he may establish his covenant which he swear unto thy fathers as it is this day.KJV*

May 31st,1981 on a Saturday night, the Lord filled me with the Holy Spirit. I had been seeking the lord for the Baptism for 5 years. I was tired and ready for the manifestation in my life. I had been fasting and praying and asking the lord to fill me. Coming home after work and hearing about a one-night church revival, I was going no matter what. I asked the lord to fill me with the Holy Ghost or else I would fast until I die. That night I was filled and began speaking in unknown tongues, the heavenly language and I could not stop. There's nothing else like it. After dismissal, I tried to talk to different ones but only tongues came forth. I went home my family was asleep. I was yet speaking. I don't know what time I went to bed that night, it was glorious, the best thing that has ever happened to me.

Since that time, I have had visions and the lord began

speaking to me. The lord said to tell others about me. I told the Lord I don't know enough about you or the bible to tell anyone anything. He said tell them what you know.

I began my prayer life. My first prayer partner was Doshie Piqee, she taught me many things how to pray. Fasting goes along with prayer. When you fast you afflict your soul. Some things come by fasting and prayer. You have to stay in fellowship with the Lord. Read your Bible, pray daily, meditate on scriptures, and pray for others especially our leaders, and family. Pray always to God be the glory for the things he has done. I give God all the credit.

I began writing in 2009. Not knowing where it would take me. The Lord was in this. I was having visions and the Lord was speaking to me. I've had just a few dreams and have seen signs and wonders that included me. One night at revival, I witnessed a man being made whole. He had one leg that was shorter than the other. After the prophetess preached the message, she made the Altar call a lot of people went to the Altar. She began praying, the power of God fell, and people were healed and delivered. As time passed, people began leaving the Altar returning to their seats. The man with short leg sat down on the front row. The servant of God went to him, he showed her his leg, you could see it was shorter than the other. She began praying for him. She prayed until the leg grew and became even with the other one. He thanked the Lord and started praising, shouting, and dancing. That was awesome to witness.

Contact Information
Annie Burton
2005 Center St
Clarksdale, MS 38614
sisterburton1@gmail.com   662-392-2869   662-985-8452

The Lord gave the word: great was the company of those that published it. Psalm 68:11

www.ingramcontent.com/pod-product-compliance
Lightning Source LLC
Chambersburg PA
CBHW052119110526
44592CB00013B/1677